WORLD SERIES CHAMPIONS
LOS ANGELES DODGERS

Published by Creative Education
P.O. Box 227, Mankato, Minnesota 56002
Creative Education is an imprint of The Creative Company
www.thecreativecompany.us

Design and production by Blue Design
Printed in the United States of America

Photographs by Corbis (Bettmann, Catherine Karnow, Chris Williams), Getty Images (Andrew
D. Bernstein, Bernstein Associates, Lisa Blumenfeld, Diamond Images, John Dominis//Time
Life Pictures, Stephen Dunn, Focus on Sport, Bob Gomel/Time & Life Pictures, Otto Greule Jr/
Stringer, Scott Halleran/Allsport, Will Hart, Ralph Morse//Time Life Pictures, National Baseball
Hall of Fame Library/MLB Photos, Olen Collection/Diamond Images, Hy Peskin//Time Life
Pictures, Photo File, Photo File/MLB Photos, Louis Requena/MLB Photos, Robert Riger, George
Silk//Time Life Pictures, Jamie Squire, William Vandivert/Time Life Pictures)

Library of Congress Cataloging-in-Publication Data

Frisch, Aaron.
Los Angeles Dodgers / by Aaron Frisch.
p. cm. — (World Series champions)
Includes index.
ISBN 978-1-58341-689-1
1. Los Angeles Dodgers (Baseball team)—History—Juvenile literature. I. Title.

GV875.L6F75 2009
796.357'640979494—dc22     2007052468

First edition
9 8 7 6 5 4 3 2 1

Cover: Outfielder Andruw Jones (top), outfielder Duke Snider (bottom)
Page 1: Pitcher Eric Gagné
Page 3: First baseman Steve Garvey

# LOS ANGELES DODGERS

## AARON FRISCH

CREATIVE EDUCATION

Shortstop Maury Wills

The Dodgers are a team in **Major League Baseball**. They play in Los Angeles, California. Los Angeles is a big city on the West Coast. It is sunny there most days.

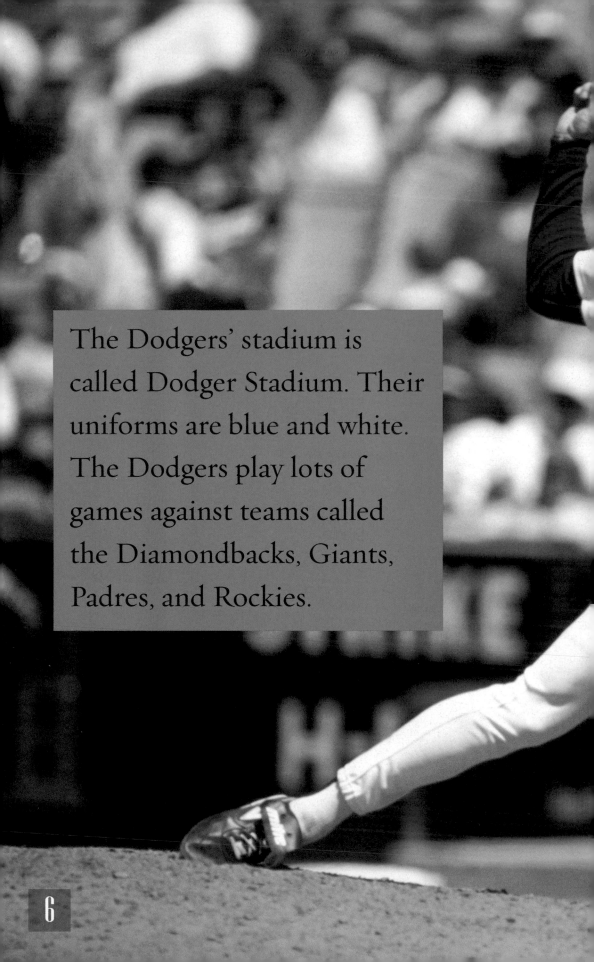

The Dodgers' stadium is called Dodger Stadium. Their uniforms are blue and white. The Dodgers play lots of games against teams called the Diamondbacks, Giants, Padres, and Rockies.

PITCHER
OREL HERSHISER

7

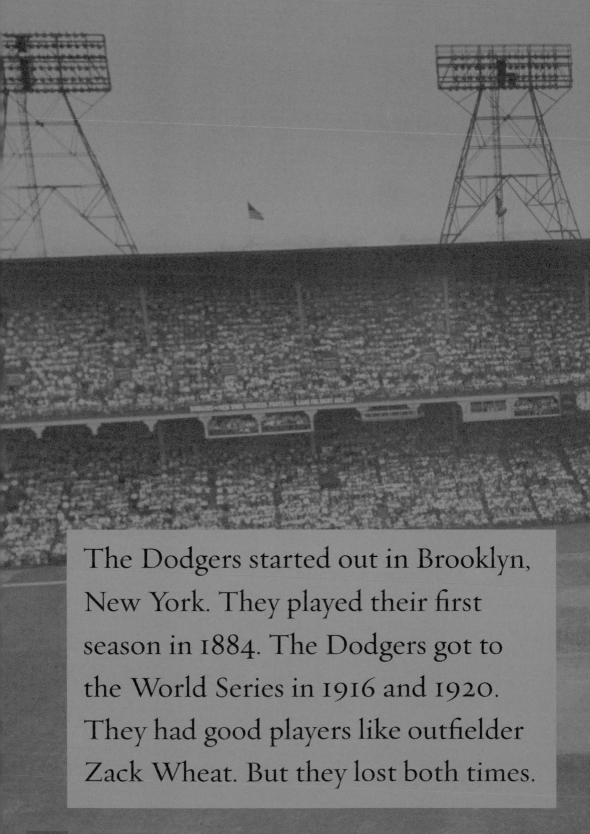

The Dodgers started out in Brooklyn, New York. They played their first season in 1884. The Dodgers got to the World Series in 1916 and 1920. They had good players like outfielder Zack Wheat. But they lost both times.

Ebbets Field in Brooklyn

# JACKIE ROBINSON

1952 Dodgers

The Dodgers were so bad in the
1930s that fans called them the "Daffy
Dodgers"! In 1947, the Dodgers got
a fast second baseman named Jackie
Robinson. He was the first black
player who got to play in the major
leagues. Robinson helped the Dodgers
get to the World Series in 1947 and
1949. But they lost both times.

PITCHER
**JOHNNY PODRES**

13

First baseman Gil Hodges

The Dodgers had lots of great players in the 1950s. Brooklyn fans cheered for players like catcher Roy Campanella and first baseman Gil Hodges. In 1955, the Dodgers finally won the World Series!

CATCHER
# ROY CAMPANELLA

Dodgers teammates

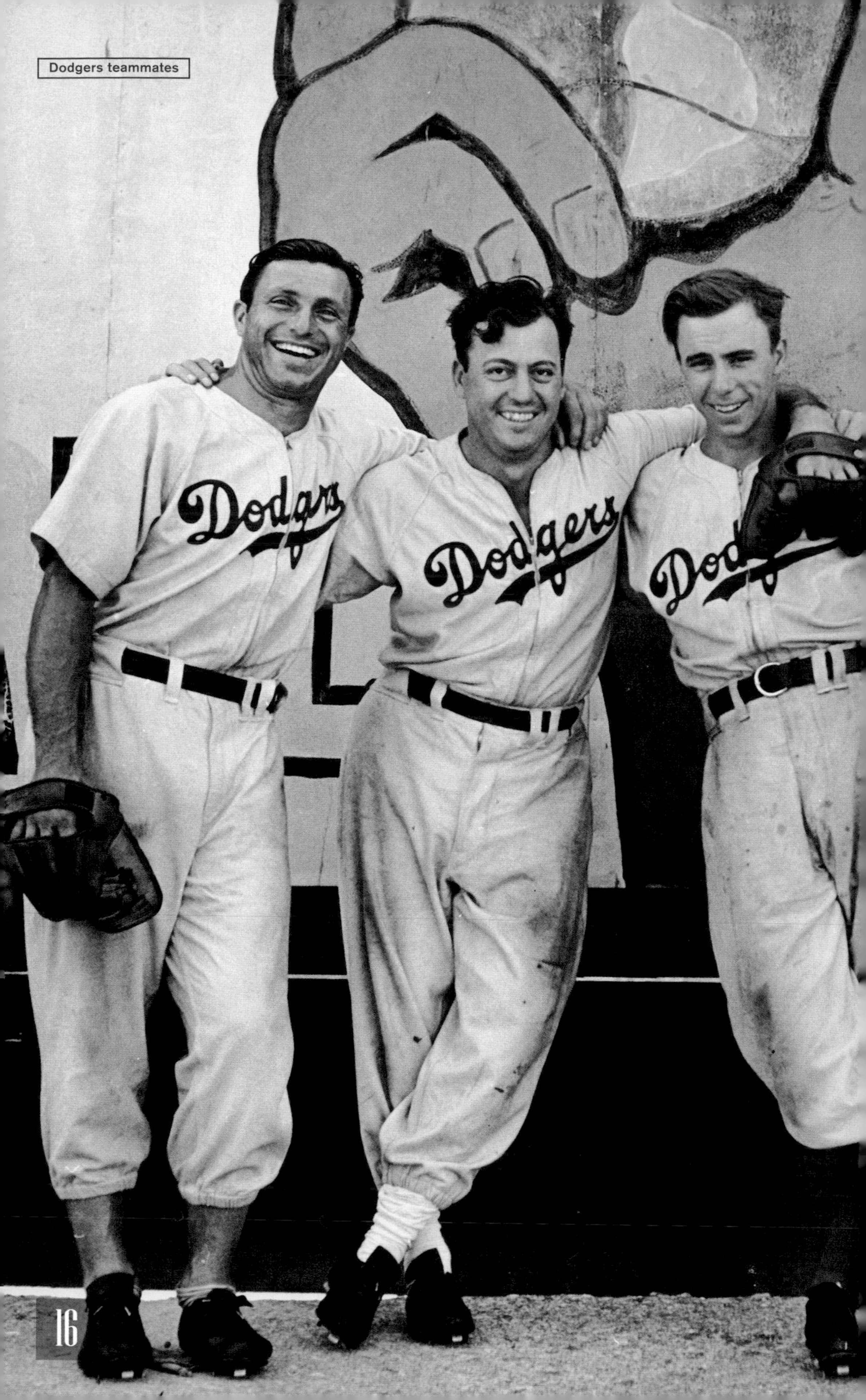

In 1958, the Dodgers moved to Los Angeles. It made Brooklyn fans sad. But Los Angeles fans liked their new team. The Dodgers won the World Series again in 1959.

# DON DRYSDALE

The Dodgers had a star pitcher named Sandy Koufax (KO-*fax*) in the 1960s. He was good at throwing **curveballs**. He helped Los Angeles win two more World Series.

# SANDY KOUFAX

MANAGER
# TOMMY LASORDA

Outfielder Kirk Gibson

Tommy Lasorda was the Dodgers' manager in the 1980s. Los Angeles won the World Series in 1981 and 1988. The Dodgers did not win any world championships after that. But they got to the **playoffs** in 2004 and 2006.

Shortstop Nomar Garciaparra

Brad Penny was another good Dodgers player. He was a big pitcher who could throw hard **fastballs**. Los Angeles fans hope that today's Dodgers will win the World Series again soon!

PITCHER
# BRAD PENNY

# GLOSSARY

**curveballs** — pitches that spin the ball and make it curve down

**fastballs** — pitches that make the ball go straight and very fast

**Major League Baseball** — a group of 30 baseball teams that play against each other; major-league teams have the best players in the world

**playoffs** — games that are played after the season to see which team is the champion

# DODGERS FACTS

**Team colors:** blue and white

**First home stadium (in Los Angeles):** Los Angeles Memorial Coliseum

**Home stadium today:** Dodger Stadium

**League/Division:** National League, Western Division

**First season in Los Angeles:** 1958

**World Series championships:** 1955, 1959, 1963, 1965, 1981, 1988

**Team name:** The Dodgers got their name because the team played games in Brooklyn near trolley tracks. A trolley is like a little train. Fans had to dodge the trolleys when they walked to the stadium.

**Major League Baseball Web site for kids:**
http://www.mlb.com/mlb/kids/

# INDEX

Brooklyn, New York 8, 11, 14, 17

Campanella, Roy 14–15

"Daffy Dodgers" 11

Dodger Stadium 6

first season 8

Hodges, Gil 14

Koufax, Sandy 18–19

Lasorda, Tommy 20–21

Penny, Brad 22–23

playoffs 21

Robinson, Jackie 10, 11

Wheat, Zack 8

World Series 8, 11, 14, 17, 18, 21